This Christmas Coloring Book
Belongs To:

____

____

Write and Draw to Express Yourself

Date: _______ / ___ / ___

Write and Draw to Express Yourself

Date: ___/___/___

Date: ___/___/___

Write and Draw to Express Yourself

Date: ___/___/___

Write and Draw to Express Yourself

Date: _____ / ___ / _____

Write and Draw to Express Yourself

Date: _______ / ___ / ___

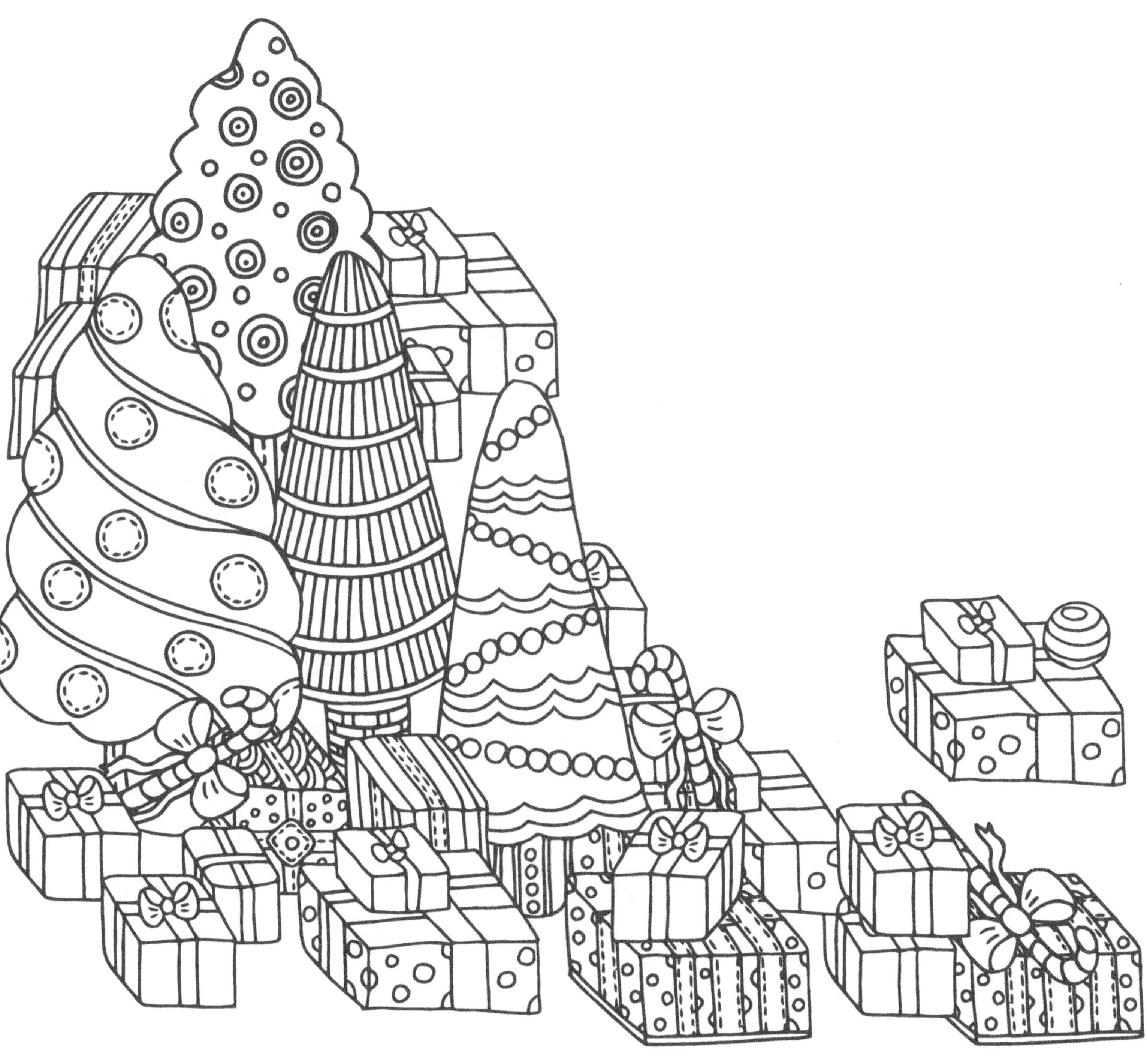

Date: _____ / ____ / _______

Write and Draw to Express Yourself

Date: ___/___/___

Write and Draw to Express Yourself

Date: _______ / ____ / ____

Date: ___ / ___ /

Write and Draw to Express Yourself

Date:
XMAS

Write and Draw to Express Yourself

Date:

Write and Draw to Express Yourself

Date: _____ / ____ / ________

Write and Draw to Express Yourself

Date: ___ / ___ / ___

Christmas Time

Date: ___ / ___ / ___

Write and Draw to Express Yourself

Date: ___ / ___ / ___

Write and Draw to Express Yourself

Write and Draw to Express Yourself

Date: _____ / ___ / ___

Write and Draw to Express Yourself

Date: ___/___/___

Write and Draw to Express Yourself

Date: ___ / ___ / ___

Date: _____ / ____ / ________

Write and Draw to Express Yourself

Date:

Write and Draw to Express Yourself

Date: ___ / ___ / ___

Write and Draw to Express Yourself

Date: _______ / ___ / ______

Write and Draw to Express Yourself

Date: ___/___/___

Write and Draw to Express Yourself

Date: ______ / ______ / ______

Date: _______ / ____ / ______

Date: ___/___/___

Write and Draw to Express Yourself

Date: ___ / ___ / ___

Date: ___/___/___

Write and Draw to Express Yourself

The
Magic of
Christmas

Write and Draw to Express Yourself

Write and Draw to Express Yourself

Date:

Write and Draw to Express Yourself

Date: ___/___/___

Write and Draw to Express Yourself

Write and Draw to Express Yourself

Date: _____ / ___ / ___

Write and Draw to Express Yourself

Date: _______/_______/_______

Date: ___/___/___

Write and Draw to Express Yourself

Date:

Write and Draw to Express Yourself

Write and Draw to Express Yourself

Write and Draw to Express Yourself

peace
&
joy

Write and Draw to Express Yourself

Date: ___ / ___ / ___

Write and Draw to Express Yourself

Write and Draw to Express Yourself

Date: ___/___/___

Write and Draw to Express Yourself

Date: _____ / ___ / _____

Date: / /

Write and Draw to Express Yourself

Date: _____ / ____ / ____

Write and Draw to Express Yourself

Date: ___/___/___

Write and Draw to Express Yourself

Date: ___/___/___